AZIMUTH

poems

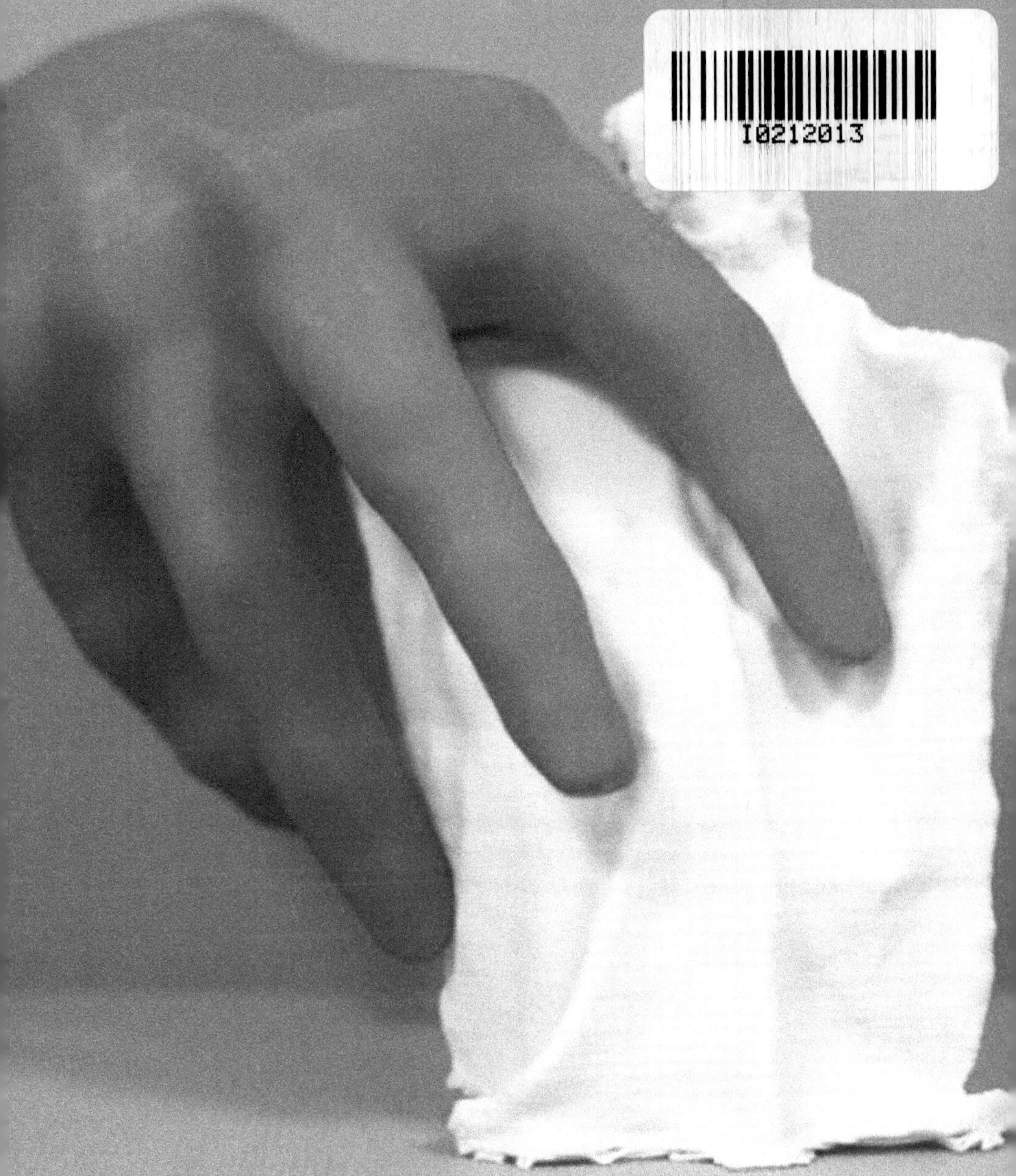

Carol Ciavonne

Azimuth

poems by

Carol Ciavonne

art by Beatriz Albuquerque

Jaded Ibis Press
sustainable literature by digital means™
an imprint of Jaded Ibis Productions

ISBN: 978-1-937543-73-0

Published by Jaded Ibis Press, *sustainable literature by digital means*™, an imprint of Jaded Ibis Productions, LLC, Seattle, Washington USA.

Cover art by Beatriz Albuquerque. Cover and book design by Debra Di Blasi.

This book is available in multiple formats, including multimedia. Visit our website for more information: jadedibisproductions.com

Thanks to the following:

D.A. Powell, dear poet, for his love and constant support, his wit and his words. To poet Patricia Hartnett, for inspiration, love and laughter. To Lois Hayna, much-honored Colorado poet, who started me on the road to publication. To Sam Witt, poet and editor, for his encouragement. To Debra Di Blasi, writer and founder of Jaded Ibis Press.

To my family: my mother, the writer who taught me literature and poetry, my father who taught me art. To my sister Mary Ann, who has always believed in me, and to Jack, Patrick and Dominic for their love. To my brother Ted, and Linda, Luke and Adriane, for their love. To my daughter Allegra, for her own talent in writing, and her help with this manuscript and others, and to Alan and Dorian. To Hody, my partner, who makes me laugh, and who has always provided a metaphorical, and often actual, room of my own for me to write and think in.

I love you all.

Additional thanks to the publications in which these poems originally appeared:

"Grief is her subject" and "Stiletto" in *New American Writing*. "Obbligato" "Quadriga" and "Conversations with Merton" in *Parcel*. "The degree of movement" in *The Journal*. "Aria" in *Pleiades*. "Fire moves over a body," and "That they themselves will be heated," in *Denver Quarterly*. "Apocalypse" in *Colorado Review*. "Apart from exotic animals" and "The foreign I" in *Lo-Ball*. "Thinking of a" in *We Are So Happy to Know Something*. "Used to like moss" in *How2*. "An animal meant" in *Boston Review*. Additionally, "Ascension in the initial v" received the Lyric Poetry Award from the Poetry Society of America and was reprinted on the PSA website at www.poetrysociety.org.

Contents

Azimuth

Quadrant

Meridian

Azimuth

Cicada

or digital clock after the nightly ritual
not knowing what you will do yourself,
to be lost, to make do with one towel,
a knife, a pan, a pot, a pen.
Tidal winds still blow inequitable,
can't talk but we know it's between us
the photos, the children, each face feral--
if you're someone else, a poster of the holy family, say,
a painting of a canyon, anything visual,
the foreignness subsides, recedes:
eardrum music, a light blue with sleep name.

Each page

foreign blank, every movement to the previous one
and the breathing to sleep. “The twittering of the
guests in the secular trees,” friend’s imitation of
tired mother fox searching for family. The future
is foreign to us. Senor Rosendo’s vatic ash
a madder for sunset; tramonto
tells where the sun goes—over the mountain
to another land, literal and yet romantic as few facts are.
What I have seen moves me.

A foreign friend

once friend, as if everyone had the same thoughts.
Some people mistake my kindness for weakness.
My conciliatory gestures for fuzzy thinking.
I want my thoughts foreign. A high plateau
where you can see for miles or clothing hanging
between buildings wherever I am. Not mistaking
bamboo for a reed, going back to check. A thing
to prepare for, to gird up. In bocca al lupo
mimicking in every language.

The house

next door where the child is the father, the baby swing
still lashed to the tree and the child walking away.
It's a chronic condition, the separation the child causes, the parent
causes. Not speaking is foreign; the tongue is bronzed. You add
to the population of devils, the dust makes it difficult to breathe.
You talk about the tv show. The father calls, the child comes to
the porch but leaves again. The steps he takes, testing how to be
a stranger, each step adds a letter.

The foreign I

spoke so slowly so slowly the person listening could not
keep listening. Halting to think, causing a lacuna, a lagoon
where another thought replaces the one that is sinking even now
and senses the impatience of the polite, taken literally: not hearing.
Xenophobia. The X makes it outside, not partaking. The accent
remains just a rough blanket, bells, the echo in the hallway,
the smell of the house.

People who live

down the street, the food tastes, the sounds at night
make me call my mother. Can't make the differentiation,
insist that the foreign is the self, as mothers do with daughters.
Subdue it, insist it is the same, memories remembered differently
by siblings; expectations don't conform to experience.
Why keep thinking as a member when the foreign shows.

And that's the foreignness of god---

even the clothing smells different, a scent
not manufactured here, at home. The impossibility
of communicating, the deliberate removal.
No openings, no letting in. Those who have least to lose
the most defensive. The forests, deserts
can't be made recognizable except by quadrant,
an inexact map. The world is too large to plot.
We are differently mad.

Before the courthouse

before the church there was blood
and blood was word. How strong a signature,
proving the eye for arch and tower, shutters,
clever cupboards. Removed from an impossible
past, an extra n, blood walks foreign on the street,
awkward, a tourist leaving before the snow,
proving to be foreign, not different.

In the idiom,

the stranger is recognized. First lesson learned.
Ca va? Ca va bien. Pablo does well but Luisa
has a cold. Imagine if it were a hard question,
a suitcase filled with seawater bilge and a gold
thread running through it. If they can get to
it. In the land of the billionaires, chase your blues
away so they don't become displaced,
imbalanced, foreign, a depth deeper than the eye,
a foggy entrance, a very small door.

In a place you know well

but the people are different and the weather is unsentimental;
a habit of mind that invites to make foreign, therefore interesting.
I recognize the differences I always knew: quiet and bells.
How can you understand the foreign if not a stranger?
Imagined antipodean tracts tell of warlike people who admire the decorative:
flowers cast in iron on cannon, the idea of honor as national placebo.
An Aurelian wall to keep in and keep safe while figuring how best
to bomb the aqueduct, or to buy the water and charge for it. What to say
of the dissociation from care that is government?
O simony, o usury, o history of the popes.

I lived in a village

with my grandparents while my parents
went to school. It wasn't like the red shoes.
The gods weren't particularly friendly. They wouldn't
speak unless you asked, but their clothes were fashionable
and any praise went to their heads. We got our history
from fiction, a hut, and the river rushed
to trade pollution for prosperity. The best
looking actors played the rebels.

Not being one thing

or another. A purgatory wherein you pray
to become entire, not preferring the moral
to the amoral, but the whole to the part.
A film about Shakers, then a film where two
people speak at once. The listener hears
the liquid quartz and the tumbled granite.
Conglomerate. In hell, there is a mountain
and a river. We'll cross that bridge at the azimuth
of love and lack. A collage can't be the one thing
a painting can.

Sleep madonna

Because we die I don't trust sleep,
haystacks like headstones, Siennese
madonnas, their gilt deciduous.
A girl on the train pulls curtains shut
on canyons. Aquarium makes a tidal sound.
Once past the Greek road, potsherds, lime and sand,
where is that place we will disembark, dormant,
where we are both at home and alone, fish and peach?

The foreign woman

The straw, the eggs. The rival peasants we all are.
Making a saint, an assimilation of the foreign. A ghost type.
Not your discontent, not the new city state.
Your house is mine, but not by rule of hospitality.
I don't trust myself to speak the language mined beneath
babbling for fluency. You whom I speak of as sympathetic
simply see the world as I do.

When I was foreign

I was galactic, elephantine; I was text
not tethered, bound, weighted. Could not reason
push from pull, no handles. I broke the latch
and could not count the coins.
Who would ask, who would ask for me?
The words I said were not the words I meant,
let awkward silence be my twin. I fit a coral
collar round my throat. Not coral, glass.
Foreign, unconsummated, my self displaced.
Not as a child knows mirror/ and this side.

Animal me

The angel gave me a little book

and I ate it.

It was sweet in my mouth

but bitter in my belly.

The angel gave me a little house.

I ate out the pith and the rind.

I was carapaced and caparisoned.

Stumbling blocks were fastened to my shins.

The angel gave me a little wound.

Like a kiss. But open.

I licked the edges and it swelled.

To recognize and to be a stranger

have the same root in Hebrew, the houses too are angles
making it difficult to sweep out the corners.
Language, explained, unfolds that which had been folded.
The corners of the rooms in the square houses unfold as dynasty.
There is no foreshadow, but the honey flows fat and sweet.
How rid yourself of the foreign? Soften the language with viscosity.
The two flows meet. Nobody goes back.

Thinking of a

scarf "azurro" misspelled, so not of the language
it purports to depict, but it is blue and should
be called "young love" for a way to name what
is lost. You can't hang on to all that past, fireplace,
a smell of piñon. We've each made our culture,
walking at night very late, three or four voices
drunk or not accustomed to accommodation.
Can't hear crickets yet, the ground too cold even
for small plastic pots.

Haven't learned

anything but cling. Not the one I wanted,
but the tree I have grown to love simply because it is mine,
those small leaves not turning red; it's the red I want, crimson,
the petals will not do to reconstruct the flower. But the quest
has got to have some heart, got to have 10,000 life-size clay warriors
if numbers mean emotion. Much in this conquering was in not
admitting the sheer dirty work of it all, in clay which can break or dissolve;
like being faced with actual photos of them, as we seldom are of soldiers.

Place that felt like

home to me was foreign, wood itself incense,
blue and yellow where sky draws
the line on the rim of the rock, each monolith.
This place where I wasn't born and didn't live.
My mother the Swede singing old songs in Spanish;
she stayed late, the banda played on.
My other self lived there, built on custom,
tiny spoon scraping the inside of the rough pot,
grainy chocolate. Who steals your history now?

In looking out

several persons are unaware of each other
but the framer or observer, the analyst or interpreter,
this perhaps, is the artist persona making decisions in retrospect.
How does one move in view of a constant observer?
Inside: the steps up and down, angles, cobbles, everyone's quarrels.
Out : red roofs, white walls, neighbors' amenities. A tranquil view,
as from a castle the peasants' huts look picturesque.
Throw out the flowers dried at the top, color faded, stems rotting
in the stew at the bottom. The believer, living in the country,
away from other people, looking back at the town, not in it or of it.

Of noble blocks and ancient grids---

di Chirico, yet art nouveau. Stunning, stupendous,
grand and grandiose. Balconies built for hoopskirts.
Neopolis, the new city, empty, people only for scale.
Ambassadors to the glass skins of the last century,
foreign to ornament. A reaction, but not mine,
my grandfather's generation, the old tired of what presents as new.
Gehry's snail curves against monolith "square" footage.
Monstrous alien altars.

An interior

grand or simple, hidden even from ourselves,
Henry James would not say, writing the thinking,
mapping the minute and inescapable. Justify. Refuse.
To be clear-eyed and willful especially ridiculous.
Then think of the illusions, much more positive:
a lagoon to dip in, paddle slowly, and always there
the wood begins to creak and split, each shift reflected
and the intervals are only as long as they can be, willful themselves.

Parting the dear objects

from their meaning endowed by one or
another, kept carefully in a drawer,
folded in tissue, or displayed on the piano,
the coins from anywhere else. This is a
film where nothing happens. The people
are polite. There's no one to root for,
no one to despise. No one is really grateful,
but no one regrets the losses. In one or two
of the objects, a snippet of shocking family
history, but that's disputed, the list of
words concrete as the litany of things.

Apart from the exotic animals

made of rust, the fountains and the grapes
of the Greeks, the unseasonable rain, we
no longer know what is foreign. As invaders
conquered Persia but became Persian, we have
become foreign imperceptibly. The continent
belongs to us. The continent belongs to
the motives of others, sometimes heartbreakingly so.
Momentary and not historical, strangers
generations hence divest, so as to go cleanly.

The body of things:

grasses   sky   people in aggregate, moving.
what is gone when the body
regains simplicity and remains to pray.
From the promontory a fault, a slip, the presence
of light and gravity, the airy measurement of
there to there on a map, or Orion as
a map of a shape, a saint explained.
Foreign no longer foreign, forgiveness no
longer necessary.

Etymology makes it like English,

a polyglot glottal stop on the way to Esperanto. A tossed salad,
a melting pot--- oh where the water is clear you can dip your shirt in---
You can't ask for the familiar, construction always going on
and police tape, pizza. There's no understanding, just acceptance.
Embraced? No. On the boat a long time, sitting at tables cheek by jowl,
the food like nothing you've tasted. Like nothing, but still food.
Still food. Still life.

Quadrant

Fire moves over a body

Fire moves over a body with a strong specific easiness
clawed, muscular, ravening;
sparse pores leave free passage
and the lack of internal cohesion permits it
to separate, easily, the particles of the body,
the last, maybe, of a species
who build with tinder, sick of
poetry and fearful.

What evolves with fire sacrifices,
so far from spring it creates its own weather.

The degree of movement necessary to birth flame

They stretched a rope over several apartments
and a street. Only seven or eight feet of the rope were
exposed to air, yet some splashes of rain fell tout a coup
(love or rage)
It is thus that a lighted pellet set on a cold metal surface
can by its internal cohesion surmount obstacles,
destroy resistances which would have been invincible,
leap instead of crawl, consume comfort,
and all that can be found there is restlessness,
the beautiful disease.

That they themselves will be heated

One who returns all the same, coming home
to find a rainy night, the smell of hearty stew.
In a movement near their axis, the clouds break,
convergent rays arrive to paint the retina chiaroscuro,
the shadowy warmth of Rembrandt
whose nose glows, a lozenge on his luminous body.
No one believes the sputtering logs will catch;
that they themselves will be heated,
the living branch
rarified to rough and silky gesture,
the family group by the fire,
other symbols.

Universe machine

The universe is a machine
artistically constructed.
    It lights up with violence,
a conflagration
in our nerves, a sensation of heat
in our eyes, matchsticks and a rag

    simple as a pulley.

Smoked like robes

A man burns a letter
supposing greater clarity
in perceiving more light.
The aether leaves its prison noisily;
words disappear but are not gone,
insinuate themselves
into pores and interstices of the body,
the palliative always emigrant.

Who resists them receives them
smoked like robes by incense.

Equilibrium

equilibrium born out of the
resistance of its surroundings
as paradox contains its contrary
sleepless into the morning.
heavy machines,
the long gone long grass of the plains,
the rectilinear.

the sun is an ardent ornament
more vehement, more porous

Can't see past

can't see past the perpetual dusk
in the foreground
or that which darkens with distance
trees like sticks of charcoal bundled into blocks.
    words become more powerful
require reading like books, pondering.

who speaks in a dark wood?
not the heart who would invite friends in
and give comfort. what speaks brings guns.

no weeping, for fear of what weeping would bring:
a beast in gaudy fur
                    one still wants to live
with the human philosophies
enameled, emboldened, polished
in terza rima.
in epics it is clearer exactly who evil is.

Used to like moss

the color of antiquity
here it signifies eating away what is
the obsession of home:
the bees have been on the cherries
now the petals fall, leaving dried stamens
that muddy the white.

In a dark wood the mockingbird sings, thinking
it is night, like babies crying from another room
when the first room is stuffed with mothers.

Burning as a direction

the trees maroon and chestnut
no light filters down
they think there will be new growth, which is the rationale for war.

difficult to walk, always having to accommodate the bones
the body does its own convincing.
some small carnival justification: the shadow of blossoms

not knowing how I got in (delusion, denial
broken shoes)
or how to go forward

thinking of
burning as a direction

Kept all her letters

kept all her letters before she disappeared
a portrait softly altered under the spotlight
and the bow still vibrating hard to describe
the way the cherry trees move in and out
of the picture, float to the foreground
recede in the next frame. No longer seeable
without blossoms, before fruit.
Symbols unreadable, glass flowers,
the little ice cold hand at the heading of the chapter.
But I reveal my unconscious.
See this picture where they all wear beaks,
clearly delighted.

Spoiled child

insomnia means danger is near
infinitely repeating
          dark dream of a spoiled child

compassion only given in the singular
and rarely   this century
I am always a little too tired
to do what is right

Lie down on the leaves; it is easier to sleep in the daytime
with my red cloak around me.

Limbo

fearing closure, the lovers become two people
who are trying to survive:
one with a coffin, one carrying a sack.
The sweetness of the notes falls on dead air.
There is rhythm because of my walking
on the leaves, reminiscent of Kurosawa's
girl and robber. Such beautiful youngsters,
needing a little shrine and a bowl of roses.

Captive to god

the hero wants to be remembered
as a physical presence
the force of bronze against the weight
of memory. Breath is distracting
it may make you grieve.
Soon I will walk out to taste the cherries
so red from the window
so tart, inedible.
All the hungry men fed after the sermon
captive to god but continuing to steal.

Grief is her subject

grief is her subject and she is subject to it

water bottled and sold at the sea. the peacock blue semi cab,

the gated community, the heritage park mall,

the Russian ballet, the sake factory, the spark arrestors.

When you live there you notice the subtitles.

Noon and five o'clock. the vintage and the asylum,

vinnie. Leaves rustled when women wore taffeta,

in asparagus spring, the grape laborious.

amoral watchers (angels)

go up in a small elevator to look down

at the pavimento notice the subtleties

infinite argument and she decked in jewels.

Revenge is her subject

revenge is her subject, entomological, intimate.

an ancient buzz.: hieroglyphic and written;

outlaw in the back room, hearing giving direction.

in the dream, she had a gold dress and the world was bigger

I had forgiven her, she was a different person: dear aunt, loving sister,

the smiling girl. not petty with suggestions, simple key scratches

the length, ballpoint pen through leather, a name on every list.

sheathed, private. drawn, public. a compound eye.

now you know nothing of my recent past

the little creatures at dusk in the illustration

red nature, sympathetic until the end.

Despair is her subject

despair is her subject; this not understood until completed. Think of Poe

or Rimbaud in a tiny room dark, the window grimed; it's cold

or thin forearm and fingers hungry in a photograph, the worn plaid dress.

Ungovernable desire. Seethe beauty as separate from sex.

In tomatoes and birds she finds it. like the word pry, so handy.

has no book no text no poem no laughing all the way to the bank.

here again she betrays her agnosticism.

mainly it's the old stuff: the dirt, the shard, the door.

Does she shut her eyes to knowledge/very well then, she...

hears jays, sees crows. bad dreams, but dreams, like the n in nulla.

The simple iron for ironing clothes. The way rock wears away skin.

inclination, from thirst.

Murder is her subject

murder is her subject, the gun, hard wood

and iron, sly. gave them one two three

not unintentional except in the timing;

beliefs so different where the commas go

and the deliberate threads, shaped and leading.

someone else's lilies press against the screen

every morning of the world, tasks, duties: prayers;

not just recording this cool skin. quotidian.

nothing classical moves me now, a purpose is not an idea.

catastrophes, there's an end to them, a crowning.

Stiletto (Archimboldo, Uccello)

wings of sulphur, the little men run
in little steps. snow. bald tires on bridges
in the south. the waterfall hums like bees
hermetic, hermit and outrage.
oh you truthteller in cloudy incarnation,
these shades mug you. murderers and the sad ones
who convince. escort, encamp, divert with fiery hair,
round horses and diagonals. all prayers like rain reversed, stiletto.

Meridian

Miniature

here you can rest with your saints in winter
the river l'hiver cold with blossoms
impastoed on bark half-plowed.
women are naked and praying in the water
"better the winter is some lenient."

a lover kneels in the cattails
behind a beehive fortress
a leopard waits in the forest
a snub-nosed jaguar, a wolf

the land converses like the monks

Ascension in the initial v

A hole, the open mouth. Can't see the back of the throat.

Placed leaves around the root to point the direction:

fathomless. Here in this specific place, but there.

St. Hilda's soul rises like smoke to heaven, from thirteen miles away.

I want to be the one who tells them at the convent,

it was a cloudy day, but I could not be mistaken,

the mist took her shape, she cupped violets to her nose.

Her eyes were full of love and morphine,

antiphonary pigments: crimson robes, the virgin's apple-green face,

indigo mantling hut and manor. Vast.

In that time, we were truly alone. A sparrow

flew in from the blizzard to shelter by the fire, then out again.

Light, heat, a momentary feast; the print of mango-colored

leaves on concrete, a graceful death leeched from them.

Apocalypse

Foure aungelis stand on the corners of the earth

holding back the four winds. the angel of order,

the angel of grace, the angel of history. the fourth angel,

waiting, in the service of. A tool, but not humble.

the angel of incidence. the angel of reflection.

Sometimes a little crazy music is called for: polyphonic bells,

every hour. Or a quartet for grief. A short piece--

to prolong it would be unbearable, reliving the instant

when the gun goes off. the end of time. eternal

compression in which the horizon extends

far white islands and the sad shacks of prisoners.

The clarinetist said the music was unplayable,

but he could play it in the future, in time,

in winter when the plum opens, auspicious;

birds so green they're gold.

Jerusalem marbled

sunset; the buildings yellow relics.
cold the only weather that counts.
a season to love, not require,
    to accustom to the draft of the fire,
the unsteady rush.
    a blade of grass becomes
a jewel becomes a forest of strange trees,
the straw grass a cutting maze knee high. The men march,
slashing and cursing, to the water's edge, to find no boats,
sun a hard ball loosely wrapped, slung low.
    beautiful David needing his scaffolding.

Quadriga St. Mark's, Venice

This half-moon bronze cast in the horse's eye, this device, this lunula,
A passion lit in the eye to animate the limbs past tide, patina,
kingdom, belief; why not in the eye of man, dull without reflection of another?
A light diffused makes the darkness stronger; chiaroscuro, the intensifying of each.
I saw the moon once in a gutter, still, wanted it still
having waited for it more formally. Lux et vita, light and life, these equations
you mediate where you are you there, in the art, in the moon, in the eye.
gods dead. but coming back.

An animal meant

an animal meant to have two horns
only has one a sack of cloth rough
a sudden collapse as if ragged brown
and canvas a hiding a hide camouflaged
large and ungainly a blunt animal
in its lungs and dry skin

If at the point where you become immersed in the thing
there's no mind and if no mind, what is necessary about
    belief, if god is an opening, if god is a divine withdrawal

The why question

The why question is never satisfactorily answered. It's a lyric story grounded. Women stay home to listen; repeated, the story grows beyond its allotment. A bone spur. Old age in a cold castle, the carpet unraveling.

the little god
inside the little god
invite
mouths open
an attention that could be listening
hope in hope out, acceptance
or something not that simple
presently at rest

I can't remember their names right now because of the singing.
The small ones where the heart and lungs are. Argue heart
as sentimental; breath is the historical context. The small clay figures
are located in the thoracic cavity, dressed festively (ceremonially, formally.)
We think memory is a place like a museum. We think like Romans.
It's hard to tell what we're waiting for.

St. Gall Patron Saint of Birds 16 October

"It is not clear why Gall is taken to be the patron of birds.
One possible reason is that it arises from a mistaken
understanding of his name, "gallo" meaning "cock" in Italian.
 Another possible origin is the legend of his exorcising
a girl of an evil spirit after two bishops had failed in an attempt.
When the saint succeeded, the demon left through
the mouth of the girl in the form of a blackbird." [1]

She tried to coax it back with a worm on her tongue,
kernels of corn. This made speech difficult. She was
forced to learn to write to communicate her needs.
After many years, she could write come back bird
in 13 languages.

Not Clear

One Possible Reason

Cock in Italian

2 Bishops Failed

Speech Difficult

Obbligato

grey is perfectly dark

the creek is frozen but the bare trees

are too graceful. There is a double fear

and a double seeking

in obedience to

obliged the long long night
            oblate

oh mother I read the Job

with the best intentions

Graceless

grace wells up; grace descends,

not moved in any way by the purely human,

my mother's ankle delicate, her foot against the pedal,

the label from a jar of curry.

grace has to be

born in lonely mountains to paint distances, but not called master,

a building with an eye that lets in light.

grace fills shallow bowls and rasps

the graceless. me, waiting.

Things

I want things. the beauty of bones, silk
and decorative. the green human presence
of utility, the lost look. because I am loved,
I can afford desire, keep it locked up.
what can you give to people you love?
they want things: all the birds that fought for fruit
in June, fig trees bound to each other by muslin.
impermanence. in the movie, the girl realizes.
only lovers can see love, the eerie light
on the cheekbones, every effortless kindness.
I am just like everyone. the smell of bread.
tomatoes, black crim and zebra,
the sediment of summer. I want things.
fuschia sky with sirocco, a fictional history.
not forgiveness; renewal.

Can you say

can you say the red patch
in the painting pulsates,
a loose net of nebulae drifts
indigo against black,
science another eye;
or bees, that one mind,
cluster and throb on the branch,
a barque sets sail, lit in the night,
free falling
what fills and empties on that plane
cast shadows pulled to breaking point,
blown like trees on the coast. they
grow in a different pattern.
each each each each
a thousand times

Aria

I.

Tenderly she almost eats fruit,
A bird in lip and tongue.
The heart is moistened and squeezed,
Chambers open onto chambers.
Hunger no longer presides;
there is thinking in the singing.

II.

Pushed mauve in midnight
insomniac, breathless.

She hears the pulse as a soft warning
under the voice.

III.

Begins with silence
and twists.
Whose grand house, whose labyrinth
made like lace but stronger leaving?
coming back
some dark strings say lost
though loss is the consolation.
who hears it makes it out to be a map.

Two kinds of blue

the bay was two kinds of blue farther,
the range between articulation and silence
the delicacy I long for
what goes over the water
and under the water
a woman crossing a bridge
an accent of yellow or red a leaf
or a scarf
deep where music is.
The Swedish soprano's heretical secret:
in order to sing you must open your throat,
cry almost
in petition and blending.

Highway

beyond the settlement lies
the country you can't see
the young like crows move backward
persons more neutral than people
wall off shadows steaming on the side of the road.
Patterns of red and yellow light
green signs words and numbers
proliferate any person written
dunn edward paints this exit
best western choices exit
the lower sky still streaked with prussian
2 stars and the shapes of trees.

Emma/water lilies

a stemmed neck
the circumference of grace
innocence in the better literature
a simple adorning nape and arch
invite all corners' contrivance
melodious
formed by the ear out of
falling and resistance
her faults would be virtues
in me
somewhere a saint rises all bones
but for red and lively tongue
clanging against the teeth

Nature exists for the excellent

"Nature exists for the excellent"
(how may we excel?)

"wrought into verbs in the language"
work and make.

The sun sets and reappears on the drive   she writes
while (time)
    a woman   looks   at
hills ice blue and representative.

A wind comes up; gold grass rattles brilliantly
over three ranges   a glow
marks the night, stuttering.

Domes

inside of domes inside my heavenly head

converts thinking. Convex arches intersect

no text, no voices. Skin sparsely wraps

bones of the face, the fingers. Dynasties

shut the oblong eyelids. Dense box

scumbled clouds fool the eye to heaven,

not trusting in the rain not coming in.

too quiet for the young, the slow march

through the squares. the half-medieval.

Daughters of empire

the daughters of empire erode

flicker between girl with braids, ram with horn.

unreadable column of accomplishments

a fixture in the world that's not modern

soaked into skin. the city is poised for rapture

stone winged and negligent

pink and yellow as the carved baby on the hill

who they say is so beautiful.

broken on broken horizon the living drown it all out

the smell of the little free seas.

Conversations with Merton

I.

grafitti on the high rise a natural erosion, not religion.

bower bird lures a sweet friend or two with borrowed plastic,

leaves in patterns. the leaf and the light behind it

fully honest each day, but each day differently:

olive and eleison.

the cells have the light that comes in modern renovations.

let me understand complexity

what looks like a dwelling place planed smooth.

II.

the voice of reason budded into the voice

I see it in small things now.

white like cherry blossoms and the sky also

is the lightest of grays. I never think I like spring

until the birds. I don't want to be silent.

the beets with their red ink that I could not peel

and the fish I could not cook. Just a phrase—

the big picture. with people my hands are dry.

III.

misunderstand me when you say god,

saints and stories of goodness for those

who can't be good. they've examined their lives.

have not. to deliver, to succumb. one lives,

millions live blotting, blurring history and future.

sound and rhythm and meaning but not told.

music is too forthcoming. strips of concrete,

unsayable art. this is what I look for and get.

IV.

doctrinaire from my bed I rise, easter green

and soil still cold. having to cross the line,

keep self from being self to learn obedience.

clean yearning obstacle. movement not monument.

the breakdown is the wanting:

she has to have or she has to love.

what about death

no one sees it thinking, so animal

training on red black and white stilts.

V.

deciding which elaborate lost symphony

walks up and down in the hospital dark,

what they call authentic, if believed.

even tourists don't want to be tourists.

maybe we can stop this, I must make evaluations.

when I didn't listen, it sounded the same,

packing interminably, a bundle of sound.

now I listen to the things I can hear.

Aftermath

The stone in spiritual understanding is the stone:

pediment, chock, impediment.

The stone in spiritual understanding is suspended.

The stone is withheld. The stone won't.

The stone is the impossibility of not thinking.

The stone is the last leap of reason.

The stone in spiritual understanding is the color red.

Nothing you see before

prepares you for the long white aftermath on the retina.

Twelve Poems for Last Year

the capacity for self deception

The cherry tree is bare and branches
like strokes of calligraphy, waves, or birds
flying upside down,W's at age eight.
Cornell's bio: insecurity, stuff.
What does it matter, one's belief in oneself?
Cornell: I wish I'd been less reserved. Me: More.

indigo is not a crutch

She says indigo addiction resolves the problem
of the painting too easily.

a three-quarters phenomenon

Silver gilt tinsel. Film
the dead tree like a live thing between two wants
and two don't wants.

what happens in ordinary life

Three martinis. A sick cat. A baby crying.
In the book the language moves like a minnow.
They're on their way north in a snowstorm.
Renascence, hands close on steering wheel.

morning leaves against window

Stop worrying about death. Bird like a broken toy
pecking on china, making the page. The red is real
in the drawing. The same ice on the wind.

plenty colonialism

but no one can see it.

plum trees appear again in my work

Paving the street, a constant beep and throb
of engine on eardrum. Weed books, only throw away two.
A conversation unwriteable as are so many things.
To put myself at risk. Keep the I out of it, cut like a pie and stretched.
The peace, I can't tell you.

I am on the planet

Somewhere stars can be watched. Refrigerator,
wind or ocean? Sun goes down oval red
in a purple fogbank, an earlier, mountainous country.

a white box of words

In spite of my horoscope, I have no successes

or failures, just sinking. In Sicily, it's gold
and rose, although in Naples more azure.

she remembers herself as more virtuous than she was

I see now how entropy works. Desire came late to many of us.
Buds like spurs, stars, something with a c.
Asterisk, an iron claw unbreakable.

it's time for cherries

A family of girls comes to ask permission
to pick the tree outside the fence. The tree
is larger, or the sunflower. Can't catch the moment
or is it lack of consciousness—it grows, but I don't comprehend it.

reading about illumination

As I was reading about illumination
the way fire is brightest at the top of the tongue,
geese flew over with no moon. The point is
the beautiful wedding favors made of bread
when time replaces money. When I sense her waiting.
Small fish viewed from above.

Afternote

Bells have an afternote of choir,
women singing a high harmonic,
fan in the back room chanting
a low note

What comes after or unintended
gives the twin, duo, duet. The bells
that put you to sleep, wake you

the quick anger of families,
open shutters, walking up steps
and down, each uneven

Wash the dishes looking out
at the corner of a building--
it fills a doorway
too deep to make round

The Bird Life

You want to know how narrow,
where the ocean is hidden
over the rise, beyond
residential where the gulls live
the bird life. Hovers. Cream.

Going against his wishes. She's
glad he's knowable. Not to visualize
the body missing or not whole,
that body she loved.

Not allowed to comment on memories,
believing doesn't change desire.
Yaw, pitch and roll.

In handing down, the handing,

brown hands, smell of soil

a clean smell. Only the colander

pricked out in little stars,

such a tiny moon.

Mourner

As in isinglass
sheets of mica, or early glass
it's there, but not clearly

in the chrysanthemum of a blizzard.
Smart animals are hiding. I know this
from the near misses--

no time to fear death when death
is upon you. Crows circle and call.
Watched for half an hour, a crow

funeral with mourners.
The woman who traces existence
sobs, screams, beats her breast.
She wears her best dress and she's hired.

Notes

"the twittering of the guests..." comes from a translated brochure for a hotel in Venice.

The idea that "to recognize" and "to be a stranger" come from the same Hebrew root came from a lecture on Ruth by Avivah Zornberg, a noted Torah scholar.

"Monstrous alien altars" comes from Henry James' The Ambassadors.

The Nature of Fire poems (Quadrant) come from the book Dissertation on the Nature of Fire and Dissertation on the Different Parts of Philosophy (my translation) by Louis de Beausobre (1753). I came by my copy by chance. The antiquity of the book itself (small as my hand, leather-bound and with the 18th century s that looks like an f) and the personality (seen in the language) of the author captivated me. The italicized language in this section is my translation.

" a beast in gaudy fur" is taken from the Hollander translation of Dante's Inferno. In a Dark Wood (Quadrant) could be considered a gloss on this work.

"foure aungelis" comes from the Wiclif translation of the Bible.

"Better the winter is some lenient," is my own translation of a latin inscription on a miniature, from Storia Della Miniatura by Sandra Vaggagini, Electa Editrice, Milano-Firenze, 1952.
The phrase "the land converses with the monks" is taken from Walter Ueberwasser's introduction to Giotto Frescoes: 17 Colour Plates, Oxford University Press, New York, Toronto, 1950.

"St. Gall" definition is taken from Butler's Lives of the Saints.

The phrase "a double fear and a double seeking" is taken from The Intimate Merton: His Life from His Journals, edited by Patrick Hart and Jonathan Montaldo, HarperCollins, San Francisco, 2001.

"Nature exists for the excellent," Ralph Waldo Emerson.

The poem Conversations with Merton was, in part, a response to ideas in essays in Merton and Sufism: The Untold Story, edited by Rob Baker and Gray Henry, Fons Vitae, Louisville, Kentucky, 1999; and essays in Merton and Hesychasm: The Prayer of the Heart, edited by Bernadette Dieker and Johnathan Montaldo, Fons Vitae, Louisville, Kentucky, 2003.

About the Poet

Carol Ciavonne is a recipient of the PSA Lyric Poetry Prize, and has published, with artist Susana Amundaraín, an art/poetry dialogue, *Birdhouse Dialogues*. She has also collaborated with Amundaraín on several theater pieces, and worked with the innovative Imaginists theater collective. Ciavonne has a B.A. in Art, and an M.A. in Poetics from New College of California. Her poems have appeared in *Denver Quarterly, Boston Review, Colorado Review, New American Writing* and *How2*, among other journals. Her essays and reviews have appeared in *Poetry Flash, Xantippe,* and *Pleiades*. She was selected as a workshop participant at the New York Center for Book Arts in 2007, and was a writer in residence at the Pécs Writers Program in Pécs, Hungary, in 2013. Ciavonne has a B.A. in Art, and an M.A. in Poetics from New College of California. She lives in Santa Rosa, California.

About the Artist

Beatriz Albuquerque was selected by *Flash Art* magazine as one of the 100 most relevant international artists under the age of 45. She is known for her interdisciplinary practices between performance and cross media. Awards include the Breakthrough Award at the 17th Biennial Cerveira; Myers Art Prize Award from Columbia University, New York; and the Premio Ambient Performance Series, PAC / edge Performance Festival, Chicago. She exhibits internationally, with solo or group exhibitions in New York, Chicago, Turkey, Brazil, Ghana, Greece, Venezuela, Portugal and elsewhere. She is the author of *ART + INTERNET + PERFORMANCE = beginning of the 90s* and *Video Games + Glitch = Learning: Video Games Vs. Teachers*. Beatriz received her MFA from The School of the Art Institute of Chicago and is currently completing her PhD in Art Education at Columbia University. She lives and works in New York and Portugal.

www.ingramcontent.com/pod-product-compliance
Lightning Source LLC
Chambersburg PA
CBHW020212090426
42734CB00008B/1033
9781937543730